My Blog Planner

Ramini Brands Book Collection
www.amazon.com/author/raminibrands

"**If you want to be a writer, you must do two things above all: Read a lot and write a lot**"

~Stephen King

Blog Planner

BLOG TITLE:

The Art of Representation

DOMAIN:

fearlessyaga.com
ByLuciadiaz.com

TARGET AUDIENCE: Grants

① Latina's wanting to build a Business

② Anyone needing Livakecthingin

DC., Maryland & Miami NYC

③ Podcast Listeners The Art of representation

NICHE OVERVIEW:

MAIN FOCUS:

This Blog is to make LUCIA Diaz a global Brand.

LUCIA DIAZ is a Latina Brand that focuses

on The Art of Representation

PRIMARY KEYWORDS: LUCIA DIAZ
The Art of Representation
Latina entrepenuer

MAIN TRAFFIC SOURCES: +Email List
+ social Media (Pintrest)

Blog Controls

ADMIN LOGIN:

AFFILIATE ACCOUNTS:

ADVERTISER ACCOUNTS:

HOSTING ACCOUNT LOGIN:

IMPORTANT Contacts

PARTNERS:

OTHER:

Social Media

TWITTER

@ hola lucia diaz

FACEBOOK

@ Fear less ya ya
hola lucia diaz

INSTAGRAM

@ hola lucia diaz

Threads

PINTEREST

@ hola Luciadiaz

OTHER

OTHER

Linkedin In ♥

OTHER

- Business Class
- We All grow Latina
- Self Made
- Luminary x AMEX
- Dale Tu Network

OTHER

Slack - Target Accelerators 4 & Alumni
- Creative Collective
- I Fund women

Brand Creation

SLOGAN / TAGLINE:

WRITING & CONTENT STYLE:

NICHE SUMMARY:

6 WORDS TO DESCRIBE MY BLOG:

HOW MY BLOG PROVIDES VALUE:

MISSION STATEMENT:

Blog Design

BLOG STYLE OBJECTIVE:

THEME USED:

BASE COLOR SCHEME:

PRIMARY FONTS USED:

LOGO / GRAPHIC DESIGNER:

DESIGN CHECKLIST:

- ✓ Verify responsive design
- Create 404 landing page
- Install contact form & opt in
- ✓ Create advertiser side widgets
- Test links in navigation menu
- ✓ Install Cookie Permission Plugin
- ✓ Install Privacy Agreement

PLUGIN CHECKLIST:

- ✓ Install SEO plugin
- Install WP Total Cache
- ✓ Install social sharing plugin
- Install WP Forms
- Install Google Analytics
- Install Backup Plugin
- Install Opt-in Plugin

Affiliate Accounts

ADVERTISER ACCOUNTS:

AFFILIATE ACCOUNTS:

Marketing Planner

TOP TRAFFIC CHANNELS:

MARKETING TO DO LIST:

FREE ADVERTISING IDEAS:

PAID ADVERTISING IDEAS:

January

TASKS, MARKETING, ENGAGEMENT & MONETIZATION

CONTENT IDEAS

- ☐ Winter Collaborations
- ☐ 26 ways creators & Artist can make money from their Art
- ☐ Grants for January

PinList

PROMOTION IDEAS

TOP PRIORITIES

- ☐ Move all IG Post to Blog worth moving

MONTHLY FOCUS

MONETIZATION IDEAS

Monthly Goals

MAIN OBJECTIVE:

GOAL:

ACTION STEPS:

GOAL:

ACTION STEPS:

GOAL:

ACTION STEPS:

TRAFFIC STATS:

MAILING LIST SUBSCRIBERS:

Content Planner

POST TITLE:

PUBLICATION DATE:

TARGETED KEYWORDS:

TO DO CHECKLIST:

- [ ] Research Topic
- [ ] Pinpoint Target Audience
- [ ] Choose target keywords
- [ ] Optimize for search engines
- [ ] Link to other blog post
- [ ] Create post images
- [ ] Proofread & Edit Post
- [ ] Schedule Post Date

SOCIAL SHARING: (circle all that apply)

TOPIC OUTLINE:

NOTES:

Content Planner

CATEGORY:

RESOURCE LINKS:

GRAPHICS/IMAGES:

KEY POINTS:

SEO CHECKLIST:

- Primary keyword in post title
- Secondary keyword in sub-title
- Keyword in first paragraph
- Word count > 1000 words
- 1-2 Outbound Links
- Internal Link Structure
- Post URL includes keywords
- Meta description added
- Post includes images
- Post includes sub-headlines
- Social sharing enabled

NOTES:

Post Planner

WEEK OF: _____

TYPE: ARTICLE: ☐ TUTORIAL: ☐ REVIEW: ☐ GUEST POST: ☐

PUBLICATION DATE:

TITLE:

CATEGORY:

KEYWORDS:

NOTES:

PUBLICATION DATE:

TITLE:

CATEGORY:

KEYWORDS:

NOTES:

PUBLICATION DATE:

TITLE:

CATEGORY:

KEYWORDS:

NOTES:

Post Planner

WEEK OF: _____

TYPE: ARTICLE: ☐   TUTORIAL: ☐   REVIEW: ☐   GUEST POST: ☐

PUBLICATION DATE:

TITLE: _____

CATEGORY: _____

KEYWORDS: _____

NOTES: _____

LIST BUILDING PROGRESS:

 # SUBSCRIBERS: _____ ☐   **EMAILED THIS WEEK** ✉

SOCIAL MEDIA PROMO THIS WEEK:

☐ 🐦   ☐ f   ☐ 𝓟   ☐ 📷   ☐ ▶   ☐ in   ☐ g+

EXTERNAL LINKS:

INTERNAL LINKS:

PRODUCTS PROMOTED:

☐ Affiliate Disclaimer Included

Guest Post Planner

POST TITLE:

PUBLISH DATE: CATEGORY:

MAIN TOPIC:

POST SUMMARY:

KEY POINTS:

☐ _____   ☐ _____

☐ _____   ☐ _____

INCLUDED LINKS: **SHARED ON:**

_____

_____   FACEBOOK ☐   INSTAGRAM ☐

_____   TWITTER ☐   PINTEREST ☐

                            ☐   ☐

TAGS & KEYWORDS: # OF COMMENTS: # OF TRACKBACKS:

_____ ☐

_____ ☐

_____ ☐   NOTES:

Marketing Planner

TOP TRAFFIC CHANNELS:

MARKETING TO DO LIST:

FREE ADVERTISING IDEAS:

PAID ADVERTISING IDEAS:

Marketing Tracker

PROMOTIONAL STRATEGIES TO MAXIMIZE EXPOSURE

PROMOTIONAL IDEAS:

MARKETING TO DO:

SOCIAL MEDIA GROWTH TRACKER:

	BEFORE:	AFTER:
f		
Instagram		
Twitter		
Pinterest		
YouTube		
OTHER:		

LIST BUILDING & ENGAGEMENT:

MAILING LIST SUBSCRIBERS:

 # OF EMAILS SENT TO SUBSCRIBERS:

 # OF NEW BLOG POSTS THIS WEEK:

 # OF COMPLETED GUEST POSTS:

NOTES:

February

TASKS, MARKETING, ENGAGEMENT & MONETIZATION

CONTENT IDEAS

PROMOTION IDEAS

TOP PRIORITIES

MONTHLY FOCUS

MONETIZATION RESOURCES

Monthly Goals

MAIN OBJECTIVE:

GOAL:

ACTION STEPS:

GOAL:

ACTION STEPS:

GOAL:

ACTION STEPS:

TRAFFIC STATS:

MAILING LIST SUBSCRIBERS:

Content Planner

POST TITLE:

PUBLICATION DATE:

TARGETED KEYWORDS:

TO DO CHECKLIST:

- Research Topic
- Pinpoint Target Audience
- Choose target keywords
- Optimize for search engines
- Link to other blog post
- Create post images
- Proofread & Edit Post
- Schedule Post Date

SOCIAL SHARING: (circle all that apply)

TOPIC OUTLINE:

NOTES:

Content Planner

CATEGORY:

RESOURCE LINKS:

GRAPHICS/IMAGES:

KEY POINTS:

SEO CHECKLIST:

- [ ] Primary keyword in post title
- [ ] Secondary keyword in sub-title
- [ ] Keyword in first paragraph
- [ ] Word count > 1000 words
- [ ] 1-2 Outbound Links
- [ ] Internal Link Structure
- [ ] Post URL includes keywords
- [ ] Meta description added
- [ ] Post includes images
- [ ] Post includes sub-headlines
- [ ] Social sharing enabled

NOTES:

Post Planner

WEEK OF: _____

TYPE: ARTICLE: ☐   TUTORIAL: ☐   REVIEW: ☐   GUEST POST: ☐

PUBLICATION DATE:

TITLE: _____

CATEGORY: _____

KEYWORDS: _____

NOTES: _____

PUBLICATION DATE:

TITLE: _____

CATEGORY: _____

KEYWORDS: _____

NOTES: _____

PUBLICATION DATE:

TITLE: _____

CATEGORY: _____

KEYWORDS: _____

NOTES: _____

Post Planner

WEEK OF: _____

TYPE: ARTICLE: ☐   TUTORIAL: ☐   REVIEW: ☐   GUEST POST: ☐

PUBLICATION DATE:

TITLE: _____

CATEGORY: _____

KEYWORDS: _____

NOTES: _____

LIST BUILDING PROGRESS:

 # SUBSCRIBERS: _____   ☐   **EMAILED THIS WEEK** ✉

SOCIAL MEDIA PROMO THIS WEEK:

☐ 🐦   ☐ f   ☐ 𝒫   ☐ 📷   ☐ ▶   ☐ in   ☐ g+

EXTERNAL LINKS:

PRODUCTS PROMOTED:

INTERNAL LINKS:

☐ Affiliate Disclaimer Included

Guest Post Planner

POST TITLE:

PUBLISH DATE: **CATEGORY:**

MAIN TOPIC:

POST SUMMARY:

KEY POINTS:

- [ ]   [ ]
- [ ]   [ ]

INCLUDED LINKS:	SHARED ON:	FACEBOOK [ ]	INSTAGRAM [ ]
		TWITTER [ ]	PINTEREST [ ]
		[ ]	[ ]

TAGS & KEYWORDS:	# OF COMMENTS:	# OF TRACKBACKS:
[ ]		
[ ]	**NOTES:**	
[ ]		

Marketing Planner

TOP TRAFFIC CHANNELS:

MARKETING TO DO LIST:

FREE ADVERTISING IDEAS:

PAID ADVERTISING IDEAS:

Marketing Tracker

PROMOTIONAL STRATEGIES TO MAXIMIZE EXPOSURE

PROMOTIONAL IDEAS:

MARKETING TO DO:

SOCIAL MEDIA GROWTH TRACKER:

	BEFORE:	AFTER:
f		
Instagram		
Twitter		
Pinterest		
YouTube		

OTHER:

LIST BUILDING & ENGAGEMENT:

MAILING LIST SUBSCRIBERS:	
# OF EMAILS SENT TO SUBSCRIBERS:	
# OF NEW BLOG POSTS THIS WEEK:	
# OF COMPLETED GUEST POSTS:	

NOTES:

March

TASKS, MARKETING, ENGAGEMENT & MONETIZATION

CONTENT IDEAS

PROMOTION IDEAS

TOP PRIORITIES

MONTHLY FOCUS

MONETIZATION RESOURCES

Monthly Goals

MAIN OBJECTIVE:

GOAL:

ACTION STEPS:

GOAL:

ACTION STEPS:

GOAL:

ACTION STEPS:

TRAFFIC STATS:

MAILING LIST SUBSCRIBERS:

Content Planner

POST TITLE:

PUBLICATION DATE:

TARGETED KEYWORDS:

TO DO CHECKLIST:

- [ ] Research Topic
- [ ] Pinpoint Target Audience
- [ ] Choose target keywords
- [ ] Optimize for search engines
- [ ] Link to other blog post
- [ ] Create post images
- [ ] Proofread & Edit Post
- [ ] Schedule Post Date

SOCIAL SHARING: (circle all that apply)

TOPIC OUTLINE:

NOTES:

Content Planner

CATEGORY:

RESOURCE LINKS:

GRAPHICS/IMAGES:

KEY POINTS:

SEO CHECKLIST:

Primary keyword in post title

Secondary keyword in sub-title

Keyword in first paragraph

Word count > 1000 words

1-2 Outbound Links

Internal Link Structure

Post URL includes keywords

Meta description added

Post includes images

Post includes sub-headlines

Social sharing enabled

NOTES:

Post Planner

WEEK OF: _____

TYPE: ARTICLE: ☐   TUTORIAL: ☐   REVIEW: ☐   GUEST POST: ☐

PUBLICATION DATE:

TITLE: _____

CATEGORY: _____

KEYWORDS: _____

NOTES: _____

PUBLICATION DATE:

TITLE: _____

CATEGORY: _____

KEYWORDS: _____

NOTES: _____

PUBLICATION DATE:

TITLE: _____

CATEGORY: _____

KEYWORDS: _____

NOTES: _____

Post Planner

WEEK OF: _____

TYPE: ARTICLE: ☐   TUTORIAL: ☐   REVIEW: ☐   GUEST POST: ☐

PUBLICATION DATE:

TITLE: _____

CATEGORY: _____

KEYWORDS: _____

NOTES:

LIST BUILDING PROGRESS:

 # SUBSCRIBERS: _____   **EMAILED THIS WEEK** ✉

SOCIAL MEDIA PROMO THIS WEEK:

☐ 🐦   ☐ f   ☐ 🅿   ☐ 📷   ☐ ▶   in   ☐ g+

EXTERNAL LINKS:

PRODUCTS PROMOTED:

INTERNAL LINKS:

Affiliate Disclaimer Included

Guest Post Planner

POST TITLE:

PUBLISH DATE:

CATEGORY:

MAIN TOPIC:

POST SUMMARY:

KEY POINTS:

INCLUDED LINKS:

SHARED ON:

FACEBOOK

INSTAGRAM

TWITTER

PINTEREST

TAGS & KEYWORDS:

OF COMMENTS:

OF TRACKBACKS:

NOTES:

Marketing Planner

TOP TRAFFIC CHANNELS:

MARKETING TO DO LIST:

FREE ADVERTISING IDEAS:

PAID ADVERTISING IDEAS:

Marketing Tracker

PROMOTIONAL STRATEGIES TO MAXIMIZE EXPOSURE

PROMOTIONAL IDEAS:

MARKETING TO DO:

SOCIAL MEDIA GROWTH TRACKER:

	BEFORE:	AFTER:
f		
Instagram		
Twitter		
Pinterest		
YouTube		
OTHER:		

LIST BUILDING & ENGAGEMENT:

MAILING LIST SUBSCRIBERS:	
# OF EMAILS SENT TO SUBSCRIBERS:	
# OF NEW BLOG POSTS THIS WEEK:	
# OF COMPLETED GUEST POSTS:	

NOTES:

April

TASKS, MARKETING, ENGAGEMENT & MONETIZATION

CONTENT IDEAS

PROMOTION IDEAS

TOP PRIORITIES

MONTHLY FOCUS

MONETIZATION RESOURCES

Monthly Goals

MAIN OBJECTIVE:

GOAL:

ACTION STEPS:

GOAL:

ACTION STEPS:

GOAL:

ACTION STEPS:

TRAFFIC STATS:

MAILING LIST SUBSCRIBERS:

Content Planner

POST TITLE:

PUBLICATION DATE:

TARGETED KEYWORDS:

TO DO CHECKLIST:

- Research Topic
- Pinpoint Target Audience
- Choose target keywords
- Optimize for search engines
- Link to other blog post
- Create post images
- Proofread & Edit Post
- Schedule Post Date

SOCIAL SHARING: (circle all that apply)

TOPIC OUTLINE:

NOTES:

Content Planner

CATEGORY:

RESOURCE LINKS:

GRAPHICS/IMAGES:

KEY POINTS:

SEO CHECKLIST:

- [ ] Primary keyword in post title
- [ ] Secondary keyword in sub-title
- [ ] Keyword in first paragraph
- [ ] Word count > 1000 words
- [ ] 1-2 Outbound Links
- [ ] Internal Link Structure
- [ ] Post URL includes keywords
- [ ] Meta description added
- [ ] Post includes images
- [ ] Post includes sub-headlines
- [ ] Social sharing enabled

NOTES:

Post Planner

WEEK OF: _____

TYPE: ARTICLE: ☐   TUTORIAL: ☐   REVIEW: ☐   GUEST POST: ☐

PUBLICATION DATE:

TITLE:

CATEGORY:

KEYWORDS:

NOTES:

PUBLICATION DATE:

TITLE:

CATEGORY:

KEYWORDS:

NOTES:

PUBLICATION DATE:

TITLE:

CATEGORY:

KEYWORDS:

NOTES:

Post Planner

WEEK OF: _____

TYPE: ARTICLE: ☐   TUTORIAL: ☐   REVIEW: ☐   GUEST POST: ☐

PUBLICATION DATE:

TITLE: _____

CATEGORY: _____

KEYWORDS: _____

NOTES: _____

_____

LIST BUILDING PROGRESS:

 # SUBSCRIBERS: _____   ☐ **EMAILED THIS WEEK** ✉

SOCIAL MEDIA PROMO THIS WEEK:

☐ 🐦   ☐ f   ☐ 𝓟   ☐ 📷   ☐ ▶   ☐ in   ☐ g+

EXTERNAL LINKS:

INTERNAL LINKS:

PRODUCTS PROMOTED:

☐ Affiliate Disclaimer Included

Guest Post Planner

POST TITLE:

PUBLISH DATE: **CATEGORY:**

MAIN TOPIC:

POST SUMMARY:

KEY POINTS:

- [ ]
- [ ]
- [ ]
- [ ]

INCLUDED LINKS:

SHARED ON:

FACEBOOK	[ ]	INSTAGRAM	[ ]
TWITTER	[ ]	PINTEREST	[ ]
	[ ]		[ ]

TAGS & KEYWORDS:

- [ ]
- [ ]
- [ ]

 # OF COMMENTS: **# OF TRACKBACKS:**

NOTES:

Marketing Planner

TOP TRAFFIC CHANNELS:

MARKETING TO DO LIST:

FREE ADVERTISING IDEAS:

PAID ADVERTISING IDEAS:

Marketing Tracker

PROMOTIONAL STRATEGIES TO MAXIMIZE EXPOSURE

PROMOTIONAL IDEAS:

MARKETING TO DO:

SOCIAL MEDIA GROWTH TRACKER:

BEFORE: AFTER:

f

O

y

P

▶

OTHER:

LIST BUILDING & ENGAGEMENT:

MAILING LIST
SUBSCRIBERS:

OF EMAILS SENT TO
SUBSCRIBERS:

OF NEW BLOG POSTS
THIS WEEK:

OF COMPLETED GUEST
POSTS:

NOTES:

May

TASKS, MARKETING, ENGAGEMENT & MONETIZATION

CONTENT IDEAS	PROMOTION IDEAS

TOP PRIORITIES

MONTHLY FOCUS	MONETIZATION RESOURCES

Monthly Goals

MAIN OBJECTIVE:

GOAL:

ACTION STEPS:

GOAL:

ACTION STEPS:

GOAL:

ACTION STEPS:

TRAFFIC STATS:

MAILING LIST SUBSCRIBERS:

Content Planner

POST TITLE:

PUBLICATION DATE:

TARGETED KEYWORDS:

TO DO CHECKLIST:

- Research Topic
- Pinpoint Target Audience
- Choose target keywords
- Optimize for search engines
- Link to other blog post
- Create post images
- Proofread & Edit Post
- Schedule Post Date

SOCIAL SHARING: (circle all that apply)

TOPIC OUTLINE:

NOTES:

Content Planner

CATEGORY:

RESOURCE LINKS:

GRAPHICS/IMAGES:

KEY POINTS:

SEO CHECKLIST:

- Primary keyword in post title
- Secondary keyword in sub-title
- Keyword in first paragraph
- Word count > 1000 words
- 1-2 Outbound Links
- Internal Link Structure
- Post URL includes keywords
- Meta description added
- Post includes images
- Post includes sub-headlines
- Social sharing enabled

NOTES:

Post Planner

WEEK OF: _____

TYPE: ARTICLE: ☐   TUTORIAL: ☐   REVIEW: ☐   GUEST POST: ☐

PUBLICATION DATE:

TITLE: _____

CATEGORY: _____

KEYWORDS: _____

NOTES: _____

PUBLICATION DATE:

TITLE: _____

CATEGORY: _____

KEYWORDS: _____

NOTES: _____

PUBLICATION DATE:

TITLE: _____

CATEGORY: _____

KEYWORDS: _____

NOTES: _____

Post Planner

WEEK OF: _____

TYPE: ARTICLE: ☐ TUTORIAL: ☐ REVIEW: ☐ GUEST POST: ☐

PUBLICATION DATE:

TITLE: _____

CATEGORY: _____

KEYWORDS: _____

NOTES: _____

LIST BUILDING PROGRESS:

SUBSCRIBERS: _____ EMAILED THIS WEEK ✉

SOCIAL MEDIA PROMO THIS WEEK:

☐ 🐦 ☐ f ☐ 🅟 ☐ 📷 ☐ ▶ ☐ in ☐ g+

EXTERNAL LINKS:

PRODUCTS PROMOTED:

INTERNAL LINKS:

☐ Affiliate Disclaimer Included

Guest Post Planner

POST TITLE:

PUBLISH DATE:

CATEGORY:

MAIN TOPIC:

POST SUMMARY:

KEY POINTS:

☐ _____ ☐ _____

☐ _____ ☐ _____

INCLUDED LINKS:

_____

_____

SHARED ON:

FACEBOOK ☐   INSTAGRAM ☐

TWITTER ☐   PINTEREST ☐

☐   ☐

TAGS & KEYWORDS:

_____ ☐

_____ ☐

_____ ☐

 # OF COMMENTS: **# OF TRACKBACKS:**

NOTES:

Marketing Planner

TOP TRAFFIC CHANNELS:

MARKETING TO DO LIST:

FREE ADVERTISING IDEAS:

PAID ADVERTISING IDEAS:

Marketing Tracker

PROMOTIONAL STRATEGIES TO MAXIMIZE EXPOSURE

PROMOTIONAL IDEAS:

MARKETING TO DO:

SOCIAL MEDIA GROWTH TRACKER:

	BEFORE:	AFTER:
f		
(Instagram)		
(Twitter)		
(Pinterest)		
(YouTube)		
OTHER:		

LIST BUILDING & ENGAGEMENT:

MAILING LIST SUBSCRIBERS:

OF EMAILS SENT TO SUBSCRIBERS:

OF NEW BLOG POSTS THIS WEEK:

OF COMPLETED GUEST POSTS:

NOTES:

June

TASKS, MARKETING, ENGAGEMENT & MONETIZATION

CONTENT IDEAS

PROMOTION IDEAS

TOP PRIORITIES

MONTHLY FOCUS

MONETIZATION RESOURCES

Monthly Goals

MAIN OBJECTIVE:

GOAL:

ACTION STEPS:

GOAL:

ACTION STEPS:

GOAL:

ACTION STEPS:

TRAFFIC STATS:

MAILING LIST SUBSCRIBERS:

Content Planner

POST TITLE:

PUBLICATION DATE:

TARGETED KEYWORDS:

TO DO CHECKLIST:

Research Topic

Pinpoint Target Audience

Choose target keywords

Optimize for search engines

Link to other blog post

SOCIAL SHARING: (circle all that apply)

Create post images

Proofread & Edit Post

Schedule Post Date

TOPIC OUTLINE:

NOTES:

Content Planner

CATEGORY:

RESOURCE LINKS:

GRAPHICS/IMAGES:

KEY POINTS:

SEO CHECKLIST:

- [ ] Primary keyword in post title
- [ ] Secondary keyword in sub-title
- [ ] Keyword in first paragraph
- [ ] Word count > 1000 words
- [ ] 1-2 Outbound Links
- [ ] Internal Link Structure
- [ ] Post URL includes keywords
- [ ] Meta description added
- [ ] Post includes images
- [ ] Post includes sub-headlines
- [ ] Social sharing enabled

NOTES:

Post Planner

WEEK OF: _____

TYPE: ARTICLE: ☐   TUTORIAL: ☐   REVIEW: ☐   GUEST POST: ☐

PUBLICATION DATE:

TITLE:

CATEGORY:

KEYWORDS:

NOTES:

PUBLICATION DATE:

TITLE:

CATEGORY:

KEYWORDS:

NOTES:

PUBLICATION DATE:

TITLE:

CATEGORY:

KEYWORDS:

NOTES:

Post Planner

WEEK OF: _____

TYPE: ARTICLE: ☐   TUTORIAL: ☐   REVIEW: ☐   GUEST POST: ☐

PUBLICATION DATE:

TITLE: _____

CATEGORY: _____

KEYWORDS: _____

NOTES: _____
_____

LIST BUILDING PROGRESS:

 # SUBSCRIBERS: _____   ☐ **EMAILED THIS WEEK** ✉

SOCIAL MEDIA PROMO THIS WEEK:

☐ 🐦   ☐ f   ☐ 𝓟   ☐ 📷   ☐ ▶   ☐ in   ☐ g+

EXTERNAL LINKS:

PRODUCTS PROMOTED:

INTERNAL LINKS:

☐ Affiliate Disclaimer Included

Guest Post Planner

POST TITLE:

PUBLISH DATE: CATEGORY:

MAIN TOPIC:

POST SUMMARY:

KEY POINTS:

INCLUDED LINKS:

SHARED ON:

FACEBOOK   INSTAGRAM

TWITTER   PINTEREST

TAGS & KEYWORDS:

OF COMMENTS: # OF TRACKBACKS:

NOTES:

Marketing Planner

TOP TRAFFIC CHANNELS:

MARKETING TO DO LIST:

FREE ADVERTISING IDEAS:

PAID ADVERTISING IDEAS:

Marketing Tracker

PROMOTIONAL IDEAS:

MARKETING TO DO:

SOCIAL MEDIA GROWTH TRACKER:

	BEFORE:	AFTER:
f		
Instagram		
Twitter		
Pinterest		
YouTube		

OTHER:

LIST BUILDING & ENGAGEMENT:

MAILING LIST SUBSCRIBERS:	
# OF EMAILS SENT TO SUBSCRIBERS:	
# OF NEW BLOG POSTS THIS WEEK:	
# OF COMPLETED GUEST POSTS:	

NOTES:

July

TASKS, MARKETING, ENGAGEMENT & MONETIZATION

CONTENT IDEAS	PROMOTION IDEAS

TOP PRIORITIES

MONTHLY FOCUS	MONETIZATION RESOURCES

Monthly Goals

GOAL:

ACTION STEPS:

GOAL:

ACTION STEPS:

GOAL:

ACTION STEPS:

TRAFFIC STATS:

MAILING LIST SUBSCRIBERS:

Content Planner

POST TITLE:

PUBLICATION DATE:

TARGETED KEYWORDS:

TO DO CHECKLIST:

- Research Topic
- Pinpoint Target Audience
- Choose target keywords
- Optimize for search engines
- Link to other blog post
- Create post images
- Proofread & Edit Post
- Schedule Post Date

SOCIAL SHARING: (circle all that apply)

TOPIC OUTLINE:

NOTES:

Content Planner

CATEGORY:

RESOURCE LINKS:

GRAPHICS/IMAGES:

KEY POINTS:

SEO CHECKLIST:

- [ ] Primary keyword in post title
- [ ] Secondary keyword in sub-title
- [ ] Keyword in first paragraph
- [ ] Word count > 1000 words
- [ ] 1-2 Outbound Links
- [ ] Internal Link Structure
- [ ] Post URL includes keywords
- [ ] Meta description added
- [ ] Post includes images
- [ ] Post includes sub-headlines
- [ ] Social sharing enabled

NOTES:

Post Planner

WEEK OF: _____

TYPE: ARTICLE: ☐   TUTORIAL: ☐   REVIEW: ☐   GUEST POST: ☐

PUBLICATION DATE:

TITLE: _____

CATEGORY: _____

KEYWORDS: _____

NOTES: _____
_____

PUBLICATION DATE:

TITLE: _____

CATEGORY: _____

KEYWORDS: _____

NOTES: _____
_____

PUBLICATION DATE:

TITLE: _____

CATEGORY: _____

KEYWORDS: _____

NOTES: _____
_____

Post Planner

WEEK OF: _____

TYPE: ARTICLE: ☐   TUTORIAL: ☐   REVIEW: ☐   GUEST POST: ☐

PUBLICATION DATE:

TITLE: _____

CATEGORY: _____

KEYWORDS: _____

NOTES: _____

_____

LIST BUILDING PROGRESS:

 # SUBSCRIBERS: _____ ☐ **EMAILED THIS WEEK** ✉

SOCIAL MEDIA PROMO THIS WEEK:

☐ 🐦   ☐ f   ☐ 📌   ☐ 📷   ☐ ▶   ☐ in   ☐ g+

EXTERNAL LINKS:

INTERNAL LINKS:

PRODUCTS PROMOTED:

☐ Affiliate Disclaimer Included

Guest Post Planner

POST TITLE:

PUBLISH DATE: CATEGORY:

MAIN TOPIC:

POST SUMMARY:

KEY POINTS:

☐ _____   ☐ _____

☐ _____   ☐ _____

INCLUDED LINKS:

_____
_____

SHARED ON:

FACEBOOK ☐   INSTAGRAM ☐

TWITTER ☐   PINTEREST ☐

☐   ☐

TAGS & KEYWORDS:

_____ ☐

_____ ☐

_____ ☐

 # OF COMMENTS: **# OF TRACKBACKS:**

NOTES:

Marketing Planner

TOP TRAFFIC CHANNELS:

MARKETING TO DO LIST:

FREE ADVERTISING IDEAS:

PAID ADVERTISING IDEAS:

Marketing Tracker

PROMOTIONAL STRATEGIES TO MAXIMIZE EXPOSURE

PROMOTIONAL IDEAS:

MARKETING TO DO:

SOCIAL MEDIA GROWTH TRACKER:

	BEFORE:	AFTER:
f		
Instagram		
Twitter		
Pinterest		
YouTube		
OTHER:		

LIST BUILDING & ENGAGEMENT:

MAILING LIST SUBSCRIBERS:	
# OF EMAILS SENT TO SUBSCRIBERS:	
# OF NEW BLOG POSTS THIS WEEK:	
# OF COMPLETED GUEST POSTS:	

NOTES:

August

TASKS, MARKETING, ENGAGEMENT & MONETIZATION

CONTENT IDEAS

PROMOTION IDEAS

TOP PRIORITIES

MONTHLY FOCUS

MONETIZATION RESOURCES

Monthly Goals

MAIN OBJECTIVE:

GOAL:

ACTION STEPS:

GOAL:

ACTION STEPS:

GOAL:

ACTION STEPS:

TRAFFIC STATS:

MAILING LIST SUBSCRIBERS:

Content Planner

POST TITLE:

PUBLICATION DATE:

TARGETED KEYWORDS:

TO DO CHECKLIST:

- [ ] Research Topic
- [ ] Pinpoint Target Audience
- [ ] Choose target keywords
- [ ] Optimize for search engines
- [ ] Link to other blog post
- [ ] Create post images
- [ ] Proofread & Edit Post
- [ ] Schedule Post Date

SOCIAL SHARING: (circle all that apply)

TOPIC OUTLINE:

NOTES:

Content Planner

CATEGORY:

RESOURCE LINKS:

GRAPHICS/IMAGES:

KEY POINTS:

SEO CHECKLIST:

- Primary keyword in post title
- Secondary keyword in sub-title
- Keyword in first paragraph
- Word count > 1000 words
- 1-2 Outbound Links
- Internal Link Structure
- Post URL includes keywords
- Meta description added
- Post includes images
- Post includes sub-headlines
- Social sharing enabled

NOTES:

Post Planner

WEEK OF: _____

TYPE: ARTICLE: ☐   TUTORIAL: ☐   REVIEW: ☐   GUEST POST: ☐

PUBLICATION DATE:

TITLE: _____

CATEGORY: _____

KEYWORDS: _____

NOTES: _____

PUBLICATION DATE:

TITLE: _____

CATEGORY: _____

KEYWORDS: _____

NOTES: _____

PUBLICATION DATE:

TITLE: _____

CATEGORY: _____

KEYWORDS: _____

NOTES: _____

Post Planner

WEEK OF: _____

TYPE: ARTICLE: ☐   TUTORIAL: ☐   REVIEW: ☐   GUEST POST: ☐

PUBLICATION DATE:

TITLE: _____

CATEGORY: _____

KEYWORDS: _____

NOTES: _____

_____

LIST BUILDING PROGRESS:

SUBSCRIBERS: _____ ☐   **EMAILED THIS WEEK** ✉

SOCIAL MEDIA PROMO THIS WEEK:

☐ 🐦   ☐ f   ☐ 𝓟   ☐ 📷   ☐ ▶   ☐ in   ☐ g+

EXTERNAL LINKS:

INTERNAL LINKS:

PRODUCTS PROMOTED:

☐ Affiliate Disclaimer Included

Guest Post Planner

POST TITLE:

PUBLISH DATE: CATEGORY:

MAIN TOPIC:

POST SUMMARY:

KEY POINTS:

INCLUDED LINKS:

SHARED ON:

FACEBOOK   INSTAGRAM

TWITTER   PINTEREST

TAGS & KEYWORDS:

OF COMMENTS: # OF TRACKBACKS:

NOTES:

Marketing Planner

TOP TRAFFIC CHANNELS:

MARKETING TO DO LIST:

FREE ADVERTISING IDEAS:

PAID ADVERTISING IDEAS:

Marketing Tracker

PROMOTIONAL STRATEGIES TO MAXIMIZE EXPOSURE

PROMOTIONAL IDEAS:

MARKETING TO DO:

SOCIAL MEDIA GROWTH TRACKER:

	BEFORE:	AFTER:
f		
Instagram		
Twitter		
Pinterest		
YouTube		
OTHER:		

LIST BUILDING & ENGAGEMENT:

MAILING LIST SUBSCRIBERS:	
# OF EMAILS SENT TO SUBSCRIBERS:	
# OF NEW BLOG POSTS THIS WEEK:	
# OF COMPLETED GUEST POSTS:	

NOTES:

September

TASKS, MARKETING, ENGAGEMENT & MONETIZATION

CONTENT IDEAS	PROMOTION IDEAS

TOP PRIORITIES

MONTHLY FOCUS	MONETIZATION RESOURCES

Monthly Goals

MAIN OBJECTIVE:

GOAL:

ACTION STEPS:

GOAL:

ACTION STEPS:

GOAL:

ACTION STEPS:

TRAFFIC STATS:

MAILING LIST SUBSCRIBERS:

Content Planner

POST TITLE:

PUBLICATION DATE:

TARGETED KEYWORDS:

TO DO CHECKLIST:

- Research Topic
- Pinpoint Target Audience
- Choose target keywords
- Optimize for search engines
- Link to other blog post
- Create post images
- Proofread & Edit Post
- Schedule Post Date

SOCIAL SHARING: (circle all that apply)

TOPIC OUTLINE:

NOTES:

Content Planner

CATEGORY:

RESOURCE LINKS:

GRAPHICS/IMAGES:

KEY POINTS:

SEO CHECKLIST:

- [ ] Primary keyword in post title
- [ ] Secondary keyword in sub-title
- [ ] Keyword in first paragraph
- [ ] Word count > 1000 words
- [ ] 1-2 Outbound Links
- [ ] Internal Link Structure
- [ ] Post URL includes keywords
- [ ] Meta description added
- [ ] Post includes images
- [ ] Post includes sub-headlines
- [ ] Social sharing enabled

NOTES:

Post Planner

WEEK OF: _____

TYPE: ARTICLE: ☐ TUTORIAL: ☐ REVIEW: ☐ GUEST POST: ☐

PUBLICATION DATE:

TITLE: _____

CATEGORY: _____

KEYWORDS: _____

NOTES: _____

_____

PUBLICATION DATE:

TITLE: _____

CATEGORY: _____

KEYWORDS: _____

NOTES: _____

_____

PUBLICATION DATE:

TITLE: _____

CATEGORY: _____

KEYWORDS: _____

NOTES: _____

_____

Post Planner

WEEK OF: _____

TYPE: ARTICLE: ☐ TUTORIAL: ☐ REVIEW: ☐ GUEST POST: ☐

PUBLICATION DATE:

TITLE: _____

CATEGORY: _____

KEYWORDS: _____

NOTES: _____

_____

LIST BUILDING PROGRESS:

SUBSCRIBERS: _____ ☐ EMAILED THIS WEEK ✉

SOCIAL MEDIA PROMO THIS WEEK:

☐ 🐦 ☐ f ☐ 𝓟 ☐ 📷 ☐ ▶ ☐ in ☐ g+

EXTERNAL LINKS:

PRODUCTS PROMOTED:

INTERNAL LINKS:

☐ Affiliate Disclaimer Included

Guest Post Planner

POST TITLE:

PUBLISH DATE: CATEGORY:

MAIN TOPIC:

POST SUMMARY:

KEY POINTS:

☐   ☐

☐   ☐

INCLUDED LINKS:

SHARED ON:

FACEBOOK ☐   INSTAGRAM ☐

TWITTER ☐   PINTEREST ☐

☐   ☐

TAGS & KEYWORDS:

☐

☐

☐

OF COMMENTS: # OF TRACKBACKS:

NOTES:

Marketing Planner

TOP TRAFFIC CHANNELS:

MARKETING TO DO LIST:

FREE ADVERTISING IDEAS:

PAID ADVERTISING IDEAS:

Marketing Tracker

PROMOTIONAL STRATEGIES TO MAXIMIZE EXPOSURE

PROMOTIONAL IDEAS:

MARKETING TO DO:

SOCIAL MEDIA GROWTH TRACKER:

	BEFORE:	AFTER:
f		
Instagram		
Twitter		
Pinterest		
YouTube		
OTHER:		

LIST BUILDING & ENGAGEMENT:

MAILING LIST SUBSCRIBERS:

OF EMAILS SENT TO SUBSCRIBERS:

OF NEW BLOG POSTS THIS WEEK:

OF COMPLETED GUEST POSTS:

NOTES:

October

TASKS, MARKETING, ENGAGEMENT & MONETIZATION

CONTENT IDEAS

PROMOTION IDEAS

TOP PRIORITIES

MONTHLY FOCUS

MONETIZATION RESOURCES

Monthly Goals

MAIN OBJECTIVE:

GOAL:

ACTION STEPS:

GOAL:

ACTION STEPS:

GOAL:

ACTION STEPS:

TRAFFIC STATS:

MAILING LIST SUBSCRIBERS:

Content Planner

POST TITLE:

PUBLICATION DATE:

TARGETED KEYWORDS:

TO DO CHECKLIST:

- Research Topic
- Pinpoint Target Audience
- Choose target keywords
- Optimize for search engines
- Link to other blog post
- Create post images
- Proofread & Edit Post
- Schedule Post Date

SOCIAL SHARING: (circle all that apply)

TOPIC OUTLINE:

NOTES:

Content Planner

CATEGORY:

RESOURCE LINKS:

GRAPHICS/IMAGES:

KEY POINTS:

SEO CHECKLIST:

- [ ] Primary keyword in post title
- [ ] Secondary keyword in sub-title
- [ ] Keyword in first paragraph
- [ ] Word count > 1000 words
- [ ] 1-2 Outbound Links
- [ ] Internal Link Structure
- [ ] Post URL includes keywords
- [ ] Meta description added
- [ ] Post includes images
- [ ] Post includes sub-headlines
- [ ] Social sharing enabled

NOTES:

Post Planner

TYPE: ARTICLE: ☐   TUTORIAL: ☐   REVIEW: ☐   GUEST POST: ☐

PUBLICATION DATE:

TITLE: _____

CATEGORY: _____

KEYWORDS: _____

NOTES: _____

_____

PUBLICATION DATE:

TITLE: _____

CATEGORY: _____

KEYWORDS: _____

NOTES: _____

_____

PUBLICATION DATE:

TITLE: _____

CATEGORY: _____

KEYWORDS: _____

NOTES: _____

_____

Post Planner

WEEK OF: _____

TYPE: ARTICLE: ☐ TUTORIAL: ☐ REVIEW: ☐ GUEST POST: ☐

PUBLICATION DATE:

TITLE: _____

CATEGORY: _____

KEYWORDS: _____

NOTES: _____

LIST BUILDING PROGRESS:

SUBSCRIBERS: _____ ☐ **EMAILED THIS WEEK** ✉

SOCIAL MEDIA PROMO THIS WEEK:

☐ 𝕏 ☐ f ☐ 𝓟 ☐ 📷 ☐ ▶ ☐ in ☐ g+

EXTERNAL LINKS:

INTERNAL LINKS:

PRODUCTS PROMOTED:

☐ Affiliate Disclaimer Included

Guest Post Planner

POST TITLE:

PUBLISH DATE: | CATEGORY:

MAIN TOPIC:

POST SUMMARY:

KEY POINTS:

- ☐
- ☐
- ☐
- ☐

INCLUDED LINKS:

SHARED ON:

FACEBOOK ☐   INSTAGRAM ☐

TWITTER ☐   PINTEREST ☐

☐   ☐

TAGS & KEYWORDS:

☐
☐
☐

OF COMMENTS: | # OF TRACKBACKS:

NOTES:

Marketing Planner

TOP TRAFFIC CHANNELS:

MARKETING TO DO LIST:

FREE ADVERTISING IDEAS:

PAID ADVERTISING IDEAS:

Marketing Tracker

PROMOTIONAL STRATEGIES TO MAXIMIZE EXPOSURE

PROMOTIONAL IDEAS:

MARKETING TO DO:

SOCIAL MEDIA GROWTH TRACKER:

	BEFORE:	AFTER:
f		
(Instagram)		
(Twitter)		
(Pinterest)		
(YouTube)		
OTHER:		

LIST BUILDING & ENGAGEMENT:

MAILING LIST SUBSCRIBERS:	
# OF EMAILS SENT TO SUBSCRIBERS:	
# OF NEW BLOG POSTS THIS WEEK:	
# OF COMPLETED GUEST POSTS:	

NOTES:

November

TASKS, MARKETING, ENGAGEMENT & MONETIZATION

CONTENT IDEAS	PROMOTION IDEAS

TOP PRIORITIES

MONTHLY FOCUS	MONETIZATION RESOURCES

Monthly Goals

MAIN OBJECTIVE:

GOAL:

ACTION STEPS:

GOAL:

ACTION STEPS:

GOAL:

ACTION STEPS:

TRAFFIC STATS:

MAILING LIST SUBSCRIBERS:

Content Planner

POST TITLE:

PUBLICATION DATE:

TARGETED KEYWORDS:

TO DO CHECKLIST:

- Research Topic
- Pinpoint Target Audience
- Choose target keywords
- Optimize for search engines
- Link to other blog post
- Create post images
- Proofread & Edit Post
- Schedule Post Date

SOCIAL SHARING: (circle all that apply)

TOPIC OUTLINE:

NOTES:

Content Planner

CATEGORY:

RESOURCE LINKS:

GRAPHICS/IMAGES:

KEY POINTS:

SEO CHECKLIST:

- Primary keyword in post title
- Secondary keyword in sub-title
- Keyword in first paragraph
- Word count > 1000 words
- 1-2 Outbound Links
- Internal Link Structure
- Post URL includes keywords
- Meta description added
- Post includes images
- Post includes sub-headlines
- Social sharing enabled

NOTES:

Post Planner

WEEK OF: _____

TYPE: ARTICLE: ☐   TUTORIAL: ☐   REVIEW: ☐   GUEST POST: ☐

PUBLICATION DATE:

TITLE: _____

CATEGORY: _____

KEYWORDS: _____

NOTES: _____

_____

PUBLICATION DATE:

TITLE: _____

CATEGORY: _____

KEYWORDS: _____

NOTES: _____

_____

PUBLICATION DATE:

TITLE: _____

CATEGORY: _____

KEYWORDS: _____

NOTES: _____

_____

Post Planner

WEEK OF: _____

TYPE: ARTICLE: ☐   TUTORIAL: ☐   REVIEW: ☐   GUEST POST: ☐

PUBLICATION DATE:

TITLE: _____

CATEGORY: _____

KEYWORDS: _____

NOTES: _____

_____

LIST BUILDING PROGRESS:

 # SUBSCRIBERS: _____ ☐   **EMAILED THIS WEEK** ✉

SOCIAL MEDIA PROMO THIS WEEK:

☐ 𝕏   ☐ f   ☐ 𝒫   ☐ ⓘ   ☐ ▶   ☐ in   ☐ 8+

EXTERNAL LINKS:

INTERNAL LINKS:

PRODUCTS PROMOTED:

☐ Affiliate Disclaimer Included

Guest Post Planner

POST TITLE:

PUBLISH DATE: CATEGORY:

MAIN TOPIC:

POST SUMMARY:

KEY POINTS:

- ☐ _____   ☐ _____
- ☐ _____   ☐ _____

INCLUDED LINKS:

_____

_____

SHARED ON:

FACEBOOK	☐	INSTAGRAM	☐
TWITTER	☐	PINTEREST	☐
	☐		☐

TAGS & KEYWORDS:

_____ ☐

_____ ☐

_____ ☐

# OF COMMENTS:	# OF TRACKBACKS:

NOTES:

Marketing Planner

TOP TRAFFIC CHANNELS:

MARKETING TO DO LIST:

FREE ADVERTISING IDEAS:

PAID ADVERTISING IDEAS:

Marketing Tracker

PROMOTIONAL STRATEGIES TO MAXIMIZE EXPOSURE

PROMOTIONAL IDEAS:

MARKETING TO DO:

SOCIAL MEDIA GROWTH TRACKER:

	BEFORE:	AFTER:
f		
Instagram		
Twitter		
Pinterest		
YouTube		

OTHER:

LIST BUILDING & ENGAGEMENT:

MAILING LIST SUBSCRIBERS:

OF EMAILS SENT TO SUBSCRIBERS:

OF NEW BLOG POSTS THIS WEEK:

OF COMPLETED GUEST POSTS:

NOTES:

December

TASKS, MARKETING, ENGAGEMENT & MONETIZATION

CONTENT IDEAS

PROMOTION IDEAS

TOP PRIORITIES

MONTHLY FOCUS

MONETIZATION RESOURCES

Monthly Goals

MAIN OBJECTIVE:

GOAL:

ACTION STEPS:

GOAL:

ACTION STEPS:

GOAL:

ACTION STEPS:

TRAFFIC STATS:

MAILING LIST SUBSCRIBERS:

Content Planner

POST TITLE:

PUBLICATION DATE:

TARGETED KEYWORDS:

TO DO CHECKLIST:

- Research Topic
- Pinpoint Target Audience
- Choose target keywords
- Optimize for search engines
- Link to other blog post
- Create post images
- Proofread & Edit Post
- Schedule Post Date

SOCIAL SHARING: (circle all that apply)

TOPIC OUTLINE:

NOTES:

Content Planner

CATEGORY:

RESOURCE LINKS:

GRAPHICS/IMAGES:

KEY POINTS:

SEO CHECKLIST:

- [ ] Primary keyword in post title
- [ ] Secondary keyword in sub-title
- [ ] Keyword in first paragraph
- [ ] Word count > 1000 words
- [ ] 1-2 Outbound Links
- [ ] Internal Link Structure
- [ ] Post URL includes keywords
- [ ] Meta description added
- [ ] Post includes images
- [ ] Post includes sub-headlines
- [ ] Social sharing enabled

NOTES:

Post Planner

WEEK OF: _____

TYPE: ARTICLE: ☐   TUTORIAL: ☐   REVIEW: ☐   GUEST POST: ☐

PUBLICATION DATE:

TITLE: _____

CATEGORY: _____

KEYWORDS: _____

NOTES: _____

PUBLICATION DATE:

TITLE: _____

CATEGORY: _____

KEYWORDS: _____

NOTES: _____

PUBLICATION DATE:

TITLE: _____

CATEGORY: _____

KEYWORDS: _____

NOTES: _____

Post Planner

WEEK OF: _____

TYPE: ARTICLE: ☐ TUTORIAL: ☐ REVIEW: ☐ GUEST POST: ☐

PUBLICATION DATE:

TITLE: _____

CATEGORY: _____

KEYWORDS: _____

NOTES: _____

LIST BUILDING PROGRESS:

 # SUBSCRIBERS: _____ ☐ **EMAILED THIS WEEK** ✉

SOCIAL MEDIA PROMO THIS WEEK:

☐ 🐦 ☐ f ☐ 📌 ☐ 📷 ☐ ▶ ☐ in ☐ g+

EXTERNAL LINKS:

INTERNAL LINKS:

PRODUCTS PROMOTED:

☐ Affiliate Disclaimer Included

Guest Post Planner

PUBLISH DATE:

CATEGORY:

MAIN TOPIC:

POST SUMMARY:

KEY POINTS:

- [ ]
- [ ]
- [ ]
- [ ]

INCLUDED LINKS:

SHARED ON:

FACEBOOK [ ]

INSTAGRAM [ ]

TWITTER [ ]

PINTEREST [ ]

[ ]

[ ]

TAGS & KEYWORDS:

- [ ]
- [ ]
- [ ]

OF COMMENTS:

OF TRACKBACKS:

NOTES:

Marketing Planner

TOP TRAFFIC CHANNELS:

MARKETING TO DO LIST:

FREE ADVERTISING IDEAS:

PAID ADVERTISING IDEAS:

Marketing Tracker

PROMOTIONAL IDEAS:

MARKETING TO DO:

SOCIAL MEDIA GROWTH TRACKER:

	BEFORE:	AFTER:
f		
ⓘ		
🐦		
𝓟		
▶		

OTHER:

LIST BUILDING & ENGAGEMENT:

MAILING LIST SUBSCRIBERS:

OF EMAILS SENT TO SUBSCRIBERS:

OF NEW BLOG POSTS THIS WEEK:

OF COMPLETED GUEST POSTS:

NOTES:

Notes

Notes

"Your brand is what other people say about you when you are not in the room."

~Jeff Bezos

Made in the USA
Middletown, DE
30 November 2022